WHERE FINBARR TAUGHT

A Concise History of Queen's/University College Cork, 1845–2006

WHERE FINBARR TAUGHT

A Concise History of Queen's/University College Cork

1845–2006

JOHN A. MURPHY

First published in 2007 by the
Office of Media and Communications
University College Cork
Ireland

A CIP catalogue record for this book is available from the British Library.

ISBN 10: 0 9552229 1 5
ISBN 13: 978 09552229 1 7

Book design and typesetting by Anú Design, Tara (www.anu-design.ie)
Printed in Ireland by ColourBooks

In memory of my parents, Thade and Nellie

Contents

Foreword

This short book is intended for the general reader interested in UCC's past. In part, it abridges my earlier work, *The College: A History of Queen's/University College Cork* (Cork, 1995), and highlights its salient points. But it also updates the story from 1995 to 2006. Those last ten years saw not just predictable growth but radical changes in UCC's fortunes. The new millennium was a catalyst in itself but there were other transforming factors at work.

There was a new awareness in government and business circles of the importance of the universities in driving the 'knowledge-based' economy and an urgent expectation of an increased academic contribution to scientific research and technological advance. The relentless pressure for further economic growth has made such advance an imperative for Irish academe, and UCC is no exception. The new talk has been of substantial postgraduate or 'fourth-level' expansion, though traditionalists fear that excessive emphasis on scientific research will be at the expense of the humanities. Like other universities, UCC believes that the conventional faculty organisation is no longer adequate for the new age and the new objectives, and has accordingly embarked on radical restructuring of the internal university framework.

All these changes are closely connected with the constitutional transformation brought about by the 1997 Universities Act which gave UCC the autonomy it had long desired and full control of its own fortunes. 1849 was the foundation, 1908 was the next milestone and the third phase has now begun. The pragmatic tone of the 1997 Act has been reflected in the managerial approach of a new UCC administration and in the business interests represented on the new governing authority. The phraseology and rhetoric of the boardroom have been evident in official documents. Meanwhile, student numbers soar (10,000 in 1993-94, 15,500 in 2004-05, a projected 21,000 in

Opposite:
The tower clock

ix

2010-11) and the student body becomes more and more culturally diversified; pro-grammes and courses proliferate; and splendid new buildings arise everywhere. An old dream is realised as an exciting city-oriented axis emerges along the north channel of the River Lee. But the new UCC also keeps faith with its past – refurbishing the Aula Maxima, conserving the Ogam and Carved Stones Collection, restoring the Crawford Observatory. And there is the startling *plus ça change* factor: is not President Kane's 'useful knowledge' concept of third-level education in 1849 essentially the same as the 'knowledge society' idea of the early 2000s?

John A. Murphy,
University College Cork, 2007

Acknowledgements

I thank Nancy Hawkes for her editorial encouragement, enthusiasm and advice, and for her skill in researching and commissioning the illustrations; Ann Geary for her skill and patience in typing an often chaotic manuscript; Andrew Bradley for his illuminating photography and UCC colleagues and officers for information and comment, particularly Professor Tom Dunne for helpful suggestions on the text.

Sources

An extensive bibliography will be found in my book, *The College: A History of Queen's/ University College Cork* (Cork University Press, 1995). For the 'additional' period up to 2006, I have used presidents' reports, UCC house publications, other information emanating from various UCC departments and sections, and newspaper articles and reports. Specialist publications that have appeared since *The College* include Frederick O'Dwyer, *The Architecture of Deane and Woodward* (Cork, 1997); Virginia Teehan and Elizabeth Wincott Heckett, *The Honan Chapel: A Golden Vision* (Cork, 2004); Damian McManus, *Ogam Stones at University College Cork* (Cork, 2004), and Denis O'Sullivan, *The Cork School of Medicine: A History* (Cork, 2007). See also John A. Murphy and Andrew Bradley, *University College Cork: A Portrait in Words and Images* (Cork, 2005), and John A. Murphy, 'The College', in *Atlas of Cork City*, ed. John Crowley *et al.* (Cork, 2005).

Academic staff, university officers and City Hall planners have generously discussed their views with me on various contemporary issues. However, the opinions expressed in these pages are entirely mine.

Illustrations

Unless otherwise indicated, photographs are by Andrew Bradley Photography, UCC Collection

ILLUSTRATIONS

Background and Beginnings

Visitors to Cork will notice the road signs proudly proclaiming 'A University City Since 1845'. That was the year legislation was enacted setting up Queen's College Cork (QCC) which some sixty years later became University College Cork (UCC). 'The College', as it is still called in popular parlance – there being no other third-level institution in the city until recent decades – opened its doors in 1849. In time, it gave Cork a distinctive academic and cultural personality and it became the focus of development in the inner western suburbs. Today it is a major generator of jobs and spending power in the urban economy and it is closely linked to industrial research and business in the region.

Why and how did all this begin? In the early nineteenth century UK context, the demand for social reform was expressed in educational terms in a move to make universities accessible to the rising professional and commercial classes. In the words of Sir Thomas Wyse MP, who was prominent in the agitation to set up a Munster college, 'to a well-educated and middle order, the State must mainly be indebted for its intellectual and moral progress'.[1] This concern for political and social stability was particularly applicable to Ireland. The Queen's Colleges initiative was partly due to the need to conciliate the Catholic middle class if social order and the union were to be preserved. That ambitious Catholic bourgeoisie, confidently emerging from the penal era, was seeking its place in the educational sun which certainly didn't shine for it in Trinity College Dublin where any welcome for non-Anglicans was limited and grudging. But providing public money for a lay Catholic university was unacceptable to the Protestant establishment and to public opinion in the UK as a

Opposite: Prison at Cork. *Steel engraving by William Henry Bartlett* c.*1840*

whole. In the end, setting up the Queen's Colleges (in Cork, Belfast and Galway) was an uneasy compromise. They would be secular in structure and ambience, religion being relegated to the private and voluntary sphere.

Curricular reform also animated the new thinking. This was seen as a move away from the privileged ivory tower of the traditional universities. Students should no longer be gentlemen of leisure but serious pursuers of active careers. QCC was to reflect these popular new values. Its first president, Sir Robert Kane, was a champion of the 'useful knowledge' philosophy. He once encouraged a young audience to emulate 'the Paladins of industry … the true heroes of the present age'.[2]

The policy-making Colleges Board asserted in 1846 that:

> for the practical wants of the middle classes, too much has been
> hitherto sacrificed to their [ancient languages] study, and that
> for a community busily occupied with practical science, with
> Commerce, with Agriculture and with manufacture, the study
> of modern languages should hold an important place.[3]

All this resonates familiarly in our own era, with its emphasis on a 'knowledge-based society'.

The general cry for wider access to a new kind of university education was given regional focus in the 1830s and early 1840s in the agitation for a third-level college in Munster. Businessmen and politicians were involved, and a leading figure was the banker James Roche, the so-called 'father of Queen's College Cork' who was to be present, to general acclaim, at the opening ceremonies and whose portrait hangs today in the vestibule in the north wing. What amounted to virtually rival committees were formed in Limerick and Cork but the better case was made for Cork. According to Sir Thomas Wyse:

> Cork is a more central situation for the Province than Limerick
> but, independent of position, it has other advantages, large
> opportunities for Medical study, for instruction in navigation,
> the Fine Arts etc.[4]

*James Roche,
chairman Munster
Colleges Committee
and so-called 'father of
Queen's College Cork'*

This view was echoed in a resolution passed at a large public meeting in 1844:

> Cork, the most populous and commercial city in the south of
> Ireland, is the appropriate site ... there already exist several
> Scientific and Literary Institutions, which present a suitable basis
> for the formation of a Provincial College in Munster.[5]

An expert observer noted:

> I do not know any city where there is a greater anxiety for really
> useful knowledge than in Cork. I attribute it very much to the
> domestic habits of the people of Cork who are fond of staying
> at home in the evening and reading ...[6]

Two prominent learned societies, the Royal Cork Institution (RCI) and the Cork
Cuvierian Society (CCS), acted as nurseries,[7] as it were, for the new college. But one of
the strongest arguments used by the Cork lobby was the existence of a well-established
tradition of medical training in the city – in fact, a ready-made 'complete School of
Medicine in full operation'.[8]

All this local agitation was important but it was the larger political and academic
considerations which led Sir Robert Peel's government to bring in the Colleges
(Ireland) Bill in the summer of 1845, setting up the new third-level institutions at
Cork, Galway and Belfast. The colleges at Cork and Galway were intended to cater
for Catholics as well as Protestants, but they were not to be Catholic colleges as
such. Queen's College Belfast, serving Protestant and Presbyterian students, would
be similarly non-denominational. Authorities in the colleges might provide facilities
for every student 'to receive religious instruction according to the creed which he pro-
fesses to hold' but no student would be compelled to attend any 'religious instruction
other than is approved by his parents or guardians'. There would be 'no religious
tests' for staff or students, and no chapels. But professors would be required to
'abstain from ... making any statement ... injurious or disrespectful to the religious
convictions of any portion of my class'. The colleges would be non-residential but

student-boarding arrangements would be supervised. Since the institutions would be publicly funded, the crown (that is, the chief secretary's office in Dublin Castle) would exercise close control, approving rules of governance and appointing presidents, professors and other college officers. Such appointments would put a premium on the loyalty of academics to the crown, that is to say, to the union.[9]

High Tories and crusading Catholics straightaway denounced the Queen's Colleges as 'godless'. The prominent prelate, Archbishop John MacHale, exhibited to them the same religious and nationalist hostility he had shown to the national schools system. The Colleges Act also provoked the opposition of the ageing Daniel O'Connell but, for Thomas Davis and Young Ireland, the 'mixed education' spirit of the act was in harmony with their fraternal national philosophy – 'combining the education of youth to secure the union of men', in Davis's words. Catholic episcopal opposition was formalised in the condemnation of the Queen's Colleges by the Synod of Thurles in 1850. Though lay involvement in the colleges was never explicitly prohibited, and attendance was never forbidden under pain of mortal sin, the general episcopal aura of disapproval was a major factor in the stagnation of the Cork and Galway colleges throughout the nineteenth century.

Queen's College Cork formally came into existence on 30 December 1845 by a royal charter of incorporation, which ordained that:

> in or near the City of Cork in our province of Munster in Ireland there shall and may be erected and established one perpetual College for students in Arts Law Physic and other useful learning which College shall be called by the name of 'Queen's College Cork' and shall consist of one president, one vice-president and such number of professors in Arts Law and Physic not exceeding Twelve in number ...[10]

The charter named Sir Robert Kane, a chemist of international renown, as the 'first and modern president' of the college. He was already president of the new Museum of Irish Industry in Dublin, afterwards the Royal College of Science. In fact, the presidency of QCC was earmarked for Kane (after whom the UCC science building

Glasshouse and
Botanical Gardens

Honan Biological Building

is now called). He was seen as a considerable catch and Sir Robert Peel thought his appointment would 'rally science around us – no bad ally'. The government also hoped that such a distinguished lay Catholic would have the best chance of 'selling' the Queen's Colleges project to official Catholic Ireland in general and to Catholic Cork and Munster in particular. As chair of the overall Colleges Board, charged with hammering out a common academic structure, Kane's role was dominant in putting flesh on the bare bones of the Colleges Act. In 1846-47, the board's work was suspended as the Famine crisis swept all other items off the agenda. Kane served on the Famine Relief Commission as well as on the health board set up to deal with the typhus outbreak. Incidentally, Keane's *The Industrial Resources of Ireland* (1844) has a prominent place in the annals of Irish economic nationalism.[11]

The Site and the Building

The 'Gillabbey site'[12] chosen as the location of QCC met with general satisfaction. The college's chief architect, Sir Thomas Deane, strongly recommended it to the Board of Works as 'excellent and commanding' and 'most beautiful for a public building'. (A Mr Denis Hayes of Blackpool Nurseries tried to secure the site for the Northside but to no avail). Deane was well aware that the planned spectacular neo-Gothic grouping of the Tower, the Library and the Aula Maxima on the cliff-edge site would have a dramatic visual impact on the spectator on the Western Road below. This was the striking prospect that greeted the young Queen Victoria during her flying visit to Cork in August 1849 (there was cholera in the city at the time): as her procession passed along the Western Road, she witnessed her statue being hoisted to the apex of the easternmost gable.

Macaulay's reference to 'a Gothic college worthy to stand in the High Street of Oxford'[13] may strike the modern Cork ear as cultural-cringish but it has been frequently quoted in guides to, and notices of, the college. Contemporary observers shared his enthusiastic admiration. In an 1874 memorial to the lord lieutenant,[14] the then president and professors expressed their concern that 'this chief public view of the College'[15] should not be obscured by the building of a continuous terrace along the Western Road in the area of what is known as Perrott's Inch. Today's environmentally conscious generation would fervently echo the professors' anxiety. Our aesthetic appreciation is further enhanced by the special nocturnal beauty afforded to the old stone by discreet and subtle floodlighting.

Opposite: The Grand View of University College Cork *by Robert Lowe Stopford*

The building was begun in 1847 and completed within two years. (The Medical

Building, parallel to but unconnected with the west wing, was built in stages between 1860 and 1880.) The manpower involved was considerable and workers from the County Cork countryside thus found some relief from the devastating consequences of the Great Famine. *The Cork Examiner* reported enthusiastically on the 'splendid structure' which was a credit 'to the artistic genius and mechanical skill of our city' and to the architect, Sir Thomas Deane – 'it gives us a satisfactory feeling of pride to say he is a Corkman'. The architectural style – variously described as Perpendicular

Gothic, Tudor Gothic and Victorian Gothic – seems to have been particularly influenced by Magdalene College, Oxford.

Why a three-sided Main Quadrangle? It has been pointed out that, at the time,
enclosed quadrangles were considered unhealthy – stale air being thought to spread
disease. But Sir Thomas Deane may well have made a deliberate design choice, feeling,
like Schubert, that it was neither necessary nor desirable to compose a closing movement. A low wall intended for the fourth side was never built. And so the light was

Right: Ornamental carvings, Main Quadrangle. Opposite page: Honorary Conferring, Aula Maxima

let flow in from the south, making the high-quality limestone quadrangle a place of soft brightness and tranquillity and, in (rare) sunshine, of basking warmth.[16] This effect is not diminished by the Boole Library, which, since the 1980s, has unobtrusively filled in the fourth side.

A remarkable feature of the quadrangle walls is the ornamental stone carvings at various points. The decorative work includes abstract figures and flowers, as well as bird, animal and human images. The tower clock, manufactured by the celebrated clockmakers and jewellers Mangans of Cork, was installed in 1851. The whole east wing of the college was given over to the president's and vice-president's houses, with a private garden behind. The north and west wings had cloisters and offices on the ground floor while the first floor accommodated lecture rooms and laboratories in the west wing and two museums in the north wing. Behind the quadrangle, on the northeast side, stood the Library and the Aula Maxima.

The Aula Maxima (literally 'greatest hall') was the largest single element in Deane and Woodward's design for the college.[17] The Board of Works schedule had called for 'a Great Hall for public purposes, distributing prizes, opening sessions, etc.' and in the architect's plan, it was called the Examination Hall. The general model was

the late medieval banqueting hall but the specific prototype appears to have been the New Hall and Library at Lincoln's Inn, opened in 1845.

In addition to its original specified uses, the Aula 'Max' has served a great many other purposes down the years. It has been a study hall, a supplementary library (from 1864), a place for presidential inaugurations and graduation ceremonies, a concerts and recitals hall, a conference centre, a banqueting room and (for a time in the late 1940s when no other suitable location on campus was available) a venue for college 'hops'. This writer can recall some far-from-fancy footwork on the knobbly pine floorboards, which, fortunately, were not a major deterrent to the blossoming of romance.

In 2000-02, UCC imaginatively undertook a major refurbishment of the Aula, costing nearly €2 million. Every feature – roof, ceiling, floor, walls, fireplaces, pendant light fittings, gallery and bookcases – was painstakingly restored and conserved, in fidelity to the original construction methods and materials. Thus, this central symbol of continuity had its integrity guaranteed for another 150 years.

Particular attention was devoted to the two impressive stained-glass windows. The window on the north wall, 'the Professor's Window', is dedicated to the memory of Robert Harkness, a Lancashire man, professor of mineralogy and geology (1853-78), who had a distinguished career as a geologist. The dominating feature of the east end of the Aula is the splendid memorial window (1866) to the great mathematician, George Boole, first professor of mathematics (1849-64). It is believed to have been inspired by Pugin's design for House of Commons windows: the lower central panel shows Boole seated, writing, with Aristotle (left) and Euclid (right) behind him. (Boolean algebra was to form the basis of computer science).

On the opposite (west) wall, hang the portraits of the successive presidents of the college, from Sir Robert Kane (1845-73) onwards. Because of the importance of the office of president, the portraits comprise a compendium of college history, or at least a significant feature of it. Sometimes facetiously referred to as 'a rogues' gallery', the display in fact includes only two rogues, the rest ranging from the mediocre to the outstanding, not forgetting the vain: one colourful president complained to the portraitist that the previous (inadequate) incumbent had been made to appear as intelligent as himself!

The Aula Maxima has been the object of superlatives from the beginning down to the present. In 1849, *The Cork Examiner* described it as 'one of the most magnificent rooms in Ireland' and remarked that the hall, with its great hammerbeam trusses, already looked mellow, although only just completed.[18] Though too small today for some conferring ceremonies, the Aula remains the iconic centre of UCC, the ceremonial and symbolic heart of the college.

Inauguration and Early Years

It was in a crowded Aula, on 7 November 1849, that Queen's College Cork was officially inaugurated. *The Cork Examiner* and the *Illustrated London News* carried reports on the 'imposing and, indeed, splendid ceremonial'. The attendance was richly representative of Cork civic and commercial life – town hailed gown in impressive numbers – and of the long-agitating Munster college lobby. 'We have sown the seed; we have awaited the growth of the plant and now we triumph in the fullness of its produce. It is for Ireland's youthful sons to reap the mental harvest.'[19]

In his two-hour(!) speech, the president, Sir Robert Kane, promised that the college would 'educate young men … for the active age and world in which we live'. Engineering and agricultural courses would provide for 'sound industrial education among the middle and higher classes of this province'. Still hopeful that Catholic Church authorities might relent in their opposition, Kane rejected the 'godless college' charge, as he was to do repeatedly thereafter, and stressed the built-in provisions for respecting and protecting religious beliefs. (UCC in the early twenty-first century is a good deal more godless than QCC was in the 1850s.) Interestingly, Kane also invoked the legend of a flourishing monastery on the Gillabbey site in Ireland's golden age. In doing so, he struck a supra-denominational note, appealed to a powerful and emotional local tradition and firmly identified the *genius loci* from that day to this:

> Fin Barra, the patron saint of Cork … left to his followers the charge of founding a seat of learning in this place: here, after nearly a thousand years, we open now the portals of this edifice and accept the task of training the youth of Munster.[20]

Opposite: Door from the President's Garden

Before long, 'where Finbarr taught, let Munster learn' was to become, and would remain, the college motto.[21]

After the inaugural celebrations, academic work commenced for the 115 students spread across the faculties of arts (including science, agriculture and engineering), law and medicine. From the outset, the governing college council had various problems to deal with. Despite QCC's scenic situation, the location had its drawbacks. The people in the immediate vicinity were 'of a very low class' with insalubrious habits, according to the professors. In particular, staff and students had to live cheek-by-jowl with the inmates of the adjoining gaol. The academics made no attempt to conceal their aversion to these neighbours from hell. The gaol and the college shared a common roadway where social undesirables congregated, particularly on the occasion of executions, which were held in public until the late 1860s. The professors, if not the students, were very distressed by 'such a painful and shocking interruption to the collegiate duties'.[22]

In the 1850s, the college authorities expressed their desire for 'a new approach' on the eastern side, which would shorten, both physically and psychologically, the distance from town. It wasn't until 1879 that a new gate, with a bridge behind, was opened on the Western Road at a point some yards to the west of the present main gates. Meanwhile there was a gateway on the College Road from 1864 but this entrance was not acceptable until the area became gentrified some time later.[23]

But all these disadvantages of class and location were overcome in time. Eventually, the physical presence of the college influenced the development of a socially desirable residential area (in the snobbish phraseology of today's property market.)

QCC suffered various tribulations during Kane's presidency. Apart from sustained Catholic episcopal disapproval, the catastrophe of the Famine affected those classes who might otherwise have been expected to support the college strongly. The absence of 'county academies' or of a secondary schools system (not available until the late 1870s) meant an inadequate intake of students attaining satisfactory matriculation standards. Other negative factors included the lack of interest among businessmen in commercial courses in the groves of academe and the absence of a requirement (in law, for example) of a university qualification for professional practice.

Sir Robert Kane was in some measure the author of his own misfortunes.[24] His

double jobbing – at the Museum of Irish Industry at UCC – made him an absentee president for much of the time. The college council accused Kane of negligence because of his protracted absences and of dictatorial intervention when in residence. He also seems to have had a temperamental difficulty in dealing with the academic staff, including George Boole. Well-publicised rows between presidents and professors, or between professors themselves, are an inescapable part of university life, or so it would seem.

It may be observed at this point that the office of president, whether in the QCC or UCC phase, has always been one of great prestige. Extramurally, the president ranks highly in the civic pecking order. Internally, he – to date, there has been no she – exercises considerable powers which have been further strengthened in our own day under the 1997 Universities Act. As real and formal academic head, the president has been more of a strong constitutional monarch than *primus inter pares*, to which role some professors would like to restrict him. As chief executive, he hires and fires

college servants. The president lived on campus down to 1954, residentially sharing the east wing, originally with the vice-president, and from the 1870s with the registrar whose office replaced that of the vice-president as second-in-command. Residency on campus enhanced the president's authoritarian role.

To return to Kane's presidency, the whole ethos of QCC became increasingly incompatible with the strengthening Catholic nationalism of the nineteenth century. With Dublin Castle firmly in command and with no community representation on the governing council, the college was seen by most Cork citizens as alien, autocratic and elitist. When a mysterious fire destroyed the west wing in 1862, the town had precious little sympathy for the badly singed gown. The investigator appointed by the Castle authorities reported that 'amongst the lower order of people here, there is no feeling of regret at the occurrence, some say it is a pity any of the building escaped'.[25]

Opposite: Clock Tower reflected in the windows of the east wing

Progress and Decline

Kane's successor, William Kirby Sullivan (president, 1873-90) brought a more 'native' character to the college.[26] Sullivan, like his predecessor, was a distinguished chemist but he was Cork-born and bred, and in close touch with local affairs. He was permanently resident on campus and this was the key to his grasp of college issues. His commitment to the institution and his vigorous direction of its development, made him one of the outstanding presidents in the whole history of the college.

Under Sullivan, the student body reached 300 in 1879-80. Of this number, 60 per cent were Catholic despite their Church's disapproval of the Queen's College. Land was acquired to secure 'free space about the college', to develop a botanic garden and plant houses and, in 1879, to make a new entrance from the Western Road. The college grounds took on the basic dimensions they were to retain up to the mid-twentieth century. Berkeley Hall (later the Honan Hostel, in turn demolished in the 1990s to make way for the extensive and multipurpose O'Rahilly Building) was opened in 1884-85 as residential accommodation for male Church of Ireland students. It was located on the corner of College Road and Donovan's Road.

Other developments in Sullivan's presidency were made possible through the beneficence of W.H. Crawford, a wealthy brewer who admired Sullivan's qualities and achievements. He was one of the few substantial benefactors in the history of the college, despite countless appeals by successive presidents for public donations. Crawford provided money for plant houses and for book acquisitions, thus enhancing the library's function as a reference resource for the south of Ireland. Moreover, he was the leading sponsor of the fine observatory built in 1880, which bears his name, and which also attracted generous funding from the Duke of Devonshire and others.

Opposite: Crawford Observatory

Crawford put up funds to enable the observatory to join a celestial photography and mapping programme and he provided a substantial sum towards the purchase of instruments. The construction of this limestone building reflected the intense contemporary public interest in astronomy and meteorology. The designer was Howard Grubb, the famous Dublin scientific instrument maker. Grubb also supplied the fittings, including the revolving telescope dome, clocks and astronomical instruments, the most important of which was an award-winning equatorially mounted telescope.

In our own day, the significance of the Crawford Observatory in architectural terms and in the history of Irish scientific technology has come to be appreciated afresh. This has been expressed in an exciting restoration project, which involves returning the observatory to full working order with an emphasis on its use as a teaching facility and as an interpretative centre for the history of Irish astronomy.[27]

The most significant development in Sullivan's presidency, in the long-term perspective, was the admission of the first women students in the 1885-86 session. The exclusively male preserve of QCC was irreversibly breached. But Catholic women were particularly pressured by their Church authorities not to attend the college, and female numbers remained tiny overall until QCC was transformed into UCC in 1908-09.

President Sullivan's comments on the pioneering women students strike the modern ear as patronising, if not sexist:

> The presence of ladies in the classrooms and the library greatly
> contributed to the preservation of order, and I expect their example
> will stimulate the men to more attentive and regular work.

Early women students experienced hostility from some chauvinist professors. The college continued to be ruled by a male establishment and, right down to the 1950s and 1960s, women students, being 'ladies', had to observe extra regulations made specially for them: they were not to smoke in public, for example, and most famously were 'not to lie about on the grass'.

Quarryman,
February 1942

In those early days, medicine was a particularly strong male monopoly. Women medical graduates struggled to get access to, and achieve equality of treatment in, posts as house doctors. However, in the early twentieth century, women began to fill academic positions in the college. A major milestone was reached with the appointment of Mary Ryan, a member of a well-known Cork merchant family, to the professorship of romance languages (1910-38), the first woman in the United Kingdom to hold a chair.

As the decades rolled on, women were employed in ever-increasing numbers on the academic staff, in the sub-professorial grades. Otherwise the college remained – and remains – a man's world at the top. All the presidents have been men, and women account for little more than 10 per cent of the professorial body.

Women students, however, impressively increased in numbers and confidence, particularly over the second half of the twentieth century. The general thrust has been towards full integration in the student body, with common students' club premises in the modern period. There were 76 women out of 430 students in 1913-14, 296 out of 906 in 1934-35, and 1165 out of 3181 in 1969-70. By then, the old patriarchal attitude in Irish society – that women's place was in the marriage market, and sending her to university (except perhaps to get a professional man) was a waste of money – had disappeared. By the late 1980s, a century after their first admission, UCC women students outnumbered men. They comprised 61 per cent of first years in 2004, and were in the majority in all the faculties except engineering.

The last decade of the nineteenth century and the first few years of the twentieth saw QCC touch rock-bottom in various ways.[28] There were two successive presidencies that turned out to be disastrous – James W. Slattery, (1890-96), and Sir Rowland Blennerhassett, (1897-1904). Both of them were perceived as creatures of government, political hacks who were rewarded with the office for services rendered. Their negligent stewardships were characterised by poor staff morale, petty wrangling, under-financing, dubious student material (an 1885 commission of inquiry heard testimony from the principals of two large city schools that the few pupils who went to the college were the backward boys of the class) and declining student numbers – 106 in 1896-97.

Opposite: In 1913–14, there were 76 women out of 430 students; by 2004 women comprised 61 per cent of first-year admissions.

A persistent negative factor was the continuing hostility of the Catholic Church authorities who were hoping to denominationalise the university system. To the Catholic nationalist population of Cork and Munster, QCC was still an alien and irrelevant institution.

The college's unsatisfactory university framework was the Royal University of Ireland (1882-1909), an examining and degree-conferring body which did not require lecture attendance at the Queen's Colleges. This arrangement had a most detrimental effect on entrance standards and student numbers at QCC. In fact, at the century's end, the college's future, if any, seemed fated to be that of a glorified medical school – in 1899 out of a total of less than 200 students, 137 were studying medicine. A 1903 visitation reported that the medical school was 'large', 'successful' and 'exceedingly well equipped'.

Visitations[29] were an interesting and regular feature of the QCC experience though they have hardly figured at all in the subsequent UCC phase. 'Ordinary' visitations were held triennially to monitor the general situation in the college. The board of visitors (predominantly, but not exclusively, composed of distinguished judges) would inspect various departments, inquire into the general state of discipline and hear appeals from any staff or student member who felt aggrieved by college treatment. An 'extraordinary' visitation could be held at any time on a particular matter either on the initiative of the visitors or on foot of an application from a professor, office-bearer or student.

Visitations were held in public, received detailed press coverage (the once-extensive media reporting of college proceedings has diminished gradually over the decades) and often aroused considerable interest. They could be seen as a kind of court of human rights. QCC was, generally speaking, an authoritarian if not an autocratic institution. In contrast, visitations were remarkably democratic, even egalitarian. Students, who were occasionally involved in serious riots and demonstrations in the 1880s and 1890s, seemed to have had no inhibitions in airing their grievances before the board of visitors and in confronting and cross-examining the president and professors.

Change and Resurgence

There was a radical change for the better in the fortunes of the college in the first two decades of the twentieth century.[30] This had to do with its constitutional transformation and also with the reforming presidency, between 1904 and 1919, of Sir Bertram Windle (knighted in 1912). Born in England, he had strong West Cork connections and was a first cousin of the writer Edith Somerville. A medical graduate of TCD, he was foremost in developing the Birmingham Medical School and the new University of Birmingham in 1900. A brilliant anatomist, he also acquired a deep interest in archaeology and became its first professor in UCC. Something of a polymath, Windle wrote and lectured on English literature, on anthropology, on education and on the relationship between Catholicism (to which he had fervently converted) and science.

Windle's appointment to QCC (through the influence of George Wyndham, the Irish chief secretary) was a signal that the meagerly endowed college was not to be downgraded, as had been feared in the prevailing atmosphere of poor morale. The new president sought to create an *esprit de corps* among students and staff alike, and was determined to establish strong links with the city. In his early president's reports, he argued the case for constitutional reform and for making the ethos and the governance of the college acceptable to majority opinion in Cork and Munster. Any solution to the long-standing Irish university question would have to be non-sectarian enough to allay the fears of English Nonconformists and Ulster Presbyterians, and yet not too secular if it was to gain the support of the Catholic bishops and lay middle class.

Opposite:
Honan Chapel

And so, TCD was left alone, Queen's College Belfast was made a university in its own right, and Cork, Dublin and Galway became the constituent colleges of the new National University of Ireland (NUI). The 1908 Irish Universities Act prefigured partition: sectarianism was institutionalised in the two new universities, north and south, despite their ostensibly non-denominational basis.

Though Windle was agitating for 'a separate and independent university' for Munster at Cork, he welcomed the 1908 act as a great step forward and he became heavily involved in drafting the statutes for the NUI and its colleges. University College Cork (UCC) received its new charter (incidentally, incorporating the principle of gender equality) in December 1908. The new governing body met on 15 December 1908 and confirmed the final orders of the now supplanted QCC college council. Indeed, continuity was indicated by the fact that the minutes of the first UCC governing body meeting appear in the same volume as the last QCC college council meeting, separated only by a page. A fine silver and enamel mace was commissioned by Windle in 1910 to symbolise the authority of the new UCC. Executed by Cork silversmith William Egan, it is a cherished item in the college treasury.

The college now entered the second phase of its history, its future assured. It had a new name (some nostalgic QCC graduates regretted the loss of the old one), a representative constitution, and a greatly extended staff. Ecclesiastical disapproval, perhaps the major factor in the college's stunted growth, was now lifted. Windle's status was much enhanced by the central role he had played in the smooth transition and he enjoyed the first conferring of NUI degrees in the Aula Maxima in 1910.

The post-1908 growth in student numbers reflected the successful turning point. There were 102 freshmen (the largest intake so far) in 1909-10 and 181 in 1910-11. The whole student body in 1900-01 had been only 171: in 1910-11, it stood at a record 404. There were new professorships: archaeology, economics, education, German, hygiene, Irish, law (common, jurisprudence and real property), mathematical physics, medical jurisprudence, music, ophthalmology and pathology. There were old professorships writ new – natural history became zoology, for example. And there were separate professorships, such as English and history, emerging from the break-up of former combined chairs. In all, this was a revolutionary expansion of academic disciplines.

Opposite: Mace-bearer, with silver and enamel ceremonial mace

However, Windle's presidency ended in disenchantment and he resigned in 1919 to take up a philosophy chair in the University of Toronto. His obsessive campaigning for an independent university – he had been frustrated by the federal shackles of the NUI (which had the final word in appointments, courses and examining) and by the perceived dominance of UCD – culminated in bitter disappointment. (It should be said that some would have seen the NUI framework as a check on Cork localism and cronyism.) Moreover, Windle's pro-British Redmondism was anathema to the resurgent Sinn Féin camp in UCC whose hostility in the end he could not live with.

Despite the unhappy conclusion of his Cork career, Bertram Windle was a great university president by any standards. (In 2004, the old medical building was fittingly named after him, and a suitable commemorative plaque unveiled.[31]) He handled the changes of his presidency with energy and skill. The combination of administrative competence and good scholarship has always marked outstanding college presidencies. He presided over an improved quality of student life, the institution of the Students' Club, the beginnings of the dental school and the reorganisation of the engineering and medical faculties.

The college premises were considerably expanded (Perrott's Inch between the river and the Western Road had been acquired in Slattery's day) particularly with the addition of the Athletic Grounds at the Mardyke in 1911 and of the Donovan's land area – on which the Dairy Science institute (now the geography building) was to be built – in 1918. The new chemistry and physics building, now housing the civil engineering department, was opened in 1911. With Windle's encouragement, the derelict Berkeley Hall was eventually developed into the Honan Hostel, a residence for Catholic men students over the following seven or eight decades.

Extramurally, Windle fulfilled the promise he had made to welcoming students on his arrival in Cork in 1904, that he would identify himself not only 'with your college, but also with the city'. He developed UCC contacts with downtown educational institutions, he fostered the first growth of adult education, he personified the town–gown fraternity of learning and he involved himself in other ways in the educational and commercial life of the region. One citizen's extravagant tribute was that Windle 'found Cork brick and he left it marble'.

During Windle's presidency, and with his active encouragement and involvement, the Honan bequest greatly enriched UCC in many ways. The Honans were a wealthy Cork merchant family whose benefactions to the college included prestige under-graduate scholarships, a biological institute, a hostel (already mentioned) and, pre-eminently, the Honan Chapel.

The chapel[32] is an exquisite example of revival Hiberno-Romanesque architecture. Modelled on such templates as Cormac's Chapel on the Rock of Cashel and St Cronan's Church at Roscrea, the Honan Chapel brilliantly reflects the best skills of the arts-and-crafts movement of the early twentieth century, a time of conscious Celtic revival. This is evident in so many beautiful features of the interior – radiant stained-glass windows, the exotic mosaics of the tiled floor, the beautiful enamelled tabernacle and the various liturgical and rubrical furnishings.

The opening of the chapel (dedicated to St Finbarr) in November 1916 signified that the new university college was at last acceptable to the Catholic bishops, though the chapel railings indicated that it was technically outside the (increasingly nominal) non-denominational institution. After Vatican II, the Honan Chapel was sensitively reordered to meet the new liturgical requirements, without in any way deviating from the integrity of the interior. Today, the chapel ecumenically serves the needs of a pluralist student body, it lends itself to musical and choral recitals and it continues to be a popular location for graduate weddings. For decades, it was physically occluded by other college buildings (including, ironically, the Honan Biological Institute) but with their recent demolition, the beautiful limestone chapel stands splendidly revealed, harmoniously flanked by the Devere Hall/Áras na Mac Léinn and by the O'Rahilly Building.

benedicite omnia opera domini domino

laudate et superexaltate eum in sæcula

Under Native Rule

There were two phases in the 'nativisation' of the college, that is to say, the transformation of what had been perceived as an alien institution into a more accessible and more representative seat of higher learning. The first step was the 1908 Irish Universities Act and the second was political independence in 1922, with a native government providing a new and favourable context for the fostering of education. (In many respects, the story of the college from 1849 to 2005 reflects the story of Ireland itself.)

In the UCC of the 1920s, there were various signs of a new self-confidence. One was the setting up of the Dairy Science institute:[33] significantly, the head of government, W.T. Cosgrave, laid the foundation stone. The institute became popular with visiting farming-related groups from all over Munster and it trained generations of creamery managers. The impressive entrance gates on the Western Road were built around the same time: symbolically, they seemed to respond to the plain citizen's aspiration to higher education. Another forward-looking initiative of a different kind was the foundation, in 1925, of Cork University Press[34] by the college's best-known figure, registrar Alfred O'Rahilly. It was the only Irish university press for most of the twentieth century and it is still flourishing in the early twenty-first. O'Rahilly was convinced that national independence must be reflected in distinctively cultural enterprises, more specifically in the stimulation of Irish learning and the provision of a publishing outlet for the researches of his fellow academics.

Another aspect of the nativising process was the Catholicising of the formally non-denominational campus. Though this had begun during Windle's presidency (quasi-public celebration of a votive or 'red' mass at commencement of the academic

Opposite: Main Gate, Western Road

year; observation of Catholic
Church holy days as college holidays), it was intensified thereafter, down to the liberal 1960s.
The October and Lenten religious retreats (separated by gender) were big college occasions,
and academic staff in their robes
participated in the annual Corpus
Christi procession downtown.
The Catholic Emancipation

*Opposite: Queen
Victoria's statue seen
from the Main Avenue
Right: Exhuming the
statue from the
President's Garden,
1995 – because of
political sensitivities,
this work was under-
taken at night*

Centenary in 1929 and the Patrician year of 1932 were fervently celebrated in the
UCC Athletic Grounds. In 1931, the academic staff, in council room assembled,
offered their 'loyal homage to our Holy Father, Pius XI'.

Throughout what might be called the decades of faith, the number of non-
Catholics in the student body was negligible. Nuns and male clerics had a substantial
presence on campus but took no part in college social life. In the governing body,
Catholic clergymen were deferred to, and there was a tradition of having priest-
lecturers, notably Capuchins, in departments such as philosophy, psychology and
sociology. A noticeable Catholic ethos permeated other departments in the humanities,
and medical ethics were Catholic medical ethics. Students were equipped through
apologetics courses to take on the enemies of the Church. The strong puritanical and
censorship mentality in Irish society generally was also reflected in college life.
Authoritarian college officers put certain library books on a restricted list, and effectively dictated to student debating societies which topics might not be discussed and
which guests might not be invited. The president's office was an effective thought-
police control point.

It has to be added that, on the one hand, the social conservatism of Cork students
facilitated this moral regime and, on the other, those who were minded to be
freethinkers had ways of evading the prevailing religiosity. But the great majority of
students, meekly accustomed to religious compliance since childhood, simply never
thought of not conforming.

5.

7.

9.

1.

The Catholic and nationalist atmosphere of UCC was strikingly illustrated by the removal in 1934 of Queen Victoria's limestone statue from the eastern pinnacle of the Aula Maxima, placed there at the opening of the college in 1849, and its replacement by a figure of St Finbarr, also carved in limestone, by the young sculptor, Séamus Murphy[35]. Thus, an 'alien' symbol gave way to an image of the saint whose monastic school was believed to have stood on a nearby site thirteen centuries earlier. In the reminiscences of one professor, what really led to Victoria's removal was the fear of the college authorities that 'republican' students would blow her up unless she was taken down. (Some years later, they were to deface the royal crest over the Arch.)

Interestingly, the downgraded statue was not destroyed but stored in an east wing office for over a decade and then interred – in 1946 – in the President's Garden! As the celebration of the 150th anniversary of the college's foundation approached, the statue was dug up, cleaned and displayed – as part of the UCC 150 Universitas exhibition – in its present Graduates Room location. Though there were some protests in Irish and

Right: Queen Victoria's statue in situ c.1934. Opposite page: St Finbarr, sculpture by Séamus Murphy, 1934. Standing seven feet high and weighing one and a half tons, it was carved in Irish limestone to harmonise with the general architectural tone of the college

Irish-American nationalist circles at the resurrection of the 'Famine Queen', wide public interest was shown in this significant reminder of the college's origins. The statue represents the thirty year-old Victoria in simple and pleasing medieval garb and she looks little the worse for wear after her long years of banishment and entombment.

Ironically, while Victoria could never be classified as 'one of our own', in the clannish Cork phrase, she was a real historical personage who visited the city albeit very briefly, whereas the reality of a historical Finbarr has been undermined by the researches of a UCC scholar (further irony) who has, even more shockingly, suggested that the saint was not a Corkman at all and never set foot in the place![36]

College, City and Region

The radical university transformation of 1908-09 and the political changes of the early 1920s did not make UCC a people's college overnight, though the governing body included members from democratically elected city and county councils throughout Munster. Employment opportunities in the college for the local community increased and UCC's significance in the local and regional economy was enhanced. Yet, in 1913, President Windle made an interesting observation that would still be true today to some extent:

> I am often surprised to find how many people in the city of Cork, educated people, who have never been inside the walls of the University College and have no idea of what kind of place it is.[37]

It was said at a Philosophical Society inaugural in 1926 that there was little or no town-gown rivalry in Cork, because town knew little of gown, and cared less.[38]

In an imaginative attempt to reach out to an apathetic community, the college arranged open days ('conversazione') in the mid-1920s, and *The Cork Examiner* reported the occasions extensively.[39] But the experiment was only moderately successful. President P.J. Merriman (1919-43) felt that 'the city had given the college the cold shoulder' and he implied that the municipal lectureship in Irish Music (later to be held by Seán Ó Riada) represented the sum total of City Hall's interest in UCC. In today's vastly changed atmosphere, annual open days draw huge and enthusiastic numbers of parents and prospective students.

Opposite: Bridge by the Main Gate

Perhaps a certain amount of town-gown tension is inescapable, and indeed healthy.[40] The determination of the citizen on the street not to be overawed by academics is expressed in a popular Cork song – 'from the courthouse to the college, there are different sorts of knowledge'. Back in the 1920s and 1930s, working-class and trade-union representatives were sensitive to perceived snubs from college personnel who were sometimes seen as aloof and snobbish. The antics of students on rag days (banned for their excesses by the college president in 1944) were not always experienced as amusing by put-upon citizens. Downtown sporting organisations felt the college was unfairly privileged when it came to competitive games. More importantly, following the popular enthusiasm in the early 1900s for university change, there was inevitable disenchantment when it turned out that the new UCC wasn't really 'the poor man's university', a phrase frequently bandied about in the pre-1908 agitation. For the plain people of Cork and Munster who couldn't afford to pay fees, scholarships were few and meagre. (Snobbery being the dominant phenomenon it is in Irish social life, children of the affluent bourgeoisie tended to look down on their scholarship-holding fellow students.) There was a widespread sense that university education was largely a process of perpetuating privilege, particularly in the medical profession. Yet the well-off in the community singularly failed to respond to the college's appeals for private benefactions.

Still, for all the negativity, there was a general civic pride in Cork's status as a university city, an increasing awareness of the college's importance to the regional economy and, from the 1920s, a gradual strengthening of the links between town and gown. A prominent city businessman, J.C. Foley, said in 1928 that 'College came down town and fraternised with the business associations'.[41] It also developed fruitful links with the School of Commerce and the Municipal Technical Institute. However, some business people had little regard for academic commerce: getting a BComm was seen as a distraction from, if not a hindrance to, a career in business.

Individual college personalities played a major part in weaving the fabric of the institution into the commercial, educational and cultural life of the city. The brilliantly unorthodox John Busteed (professor of economics, 1924-64) almost single-handedly got downtown commerce to take UCC seriously. He was a highly popular lecturer in adult education courses.[42]

The dynamic Alfred O'Rahilly[43] (registrar, 1920-43; president, 1943-54) preached the gospel of Cork's economic and industrial expansion. He had served on the city council in the heroic age of Tomás MacCurtain and Terence MacSwiney and had represented the city for a year in Dáil Éireann. His links with local labour were long and close, and his diary was crowded with downtown speaking appearances. He promoted the extension lecture system and pioneered diploma courses in adult education, which greatly helped to fulfil the declared objective of the UCC governing body in 1910 to extend 'the sphere of usefulness throughout Munster'.

But the academic name above all others in the twentieth century which epitomised UCC's service to the community was that of Aloys Fleischmann (professor of music, 1936-80).[44] He worked unstintingly, and well after retirement, to promote orchestral, choral and ballet music among the people of Cork and to bring musicians of international repute to the city. The ongoing success of the Cork International Choral Festival is a living memorial to his achievements.

The deepening integration of the town-gown relationship in recent decades can be seen in one sense as part of a modernisation process both in the university and in society at large. For one thing, government and society now expect universities to be accountable to the wider community. Also, the democratisation of student intake (aided by an extensive widening of the grants system) has meant a huge increase in student and staff numbers. This development, in turn, has further boosted the regional economy in terms of jobs and services and has also led to more and more acquisition of former residential property in the vicinity of the campus.

Closer college-community contacts have admittedly caused some problems: neighbourhood residents have complained about student behaviour in suburban flatlands, about obstructive parking and about restricted vistas due to new college buildings.

The revival of rag days was not universally welcomed downtown and boisterous students were famously denounced by the lord mayor in 1981 as 'subsidised brats'. Steps taken by the college in the late 1980s to extricate itself from involvement in

Previous page:
Mardyke Arena

the Fota estate[45] constituted a public relations debacle. But valuable lessons were learned from this episode and the UCC authorities acquainted themselves perforce with the unfamiliar art of diplomacy. Overall, a remarkable harmony prevails at present between town and gown.

The raising of educational standards in the general population has meant an increasing demand for UCC-led direction of various educational services, for expert college advice in various areas and for the provision of public lectures and seminars by dynamic college departments. For example, expertise in changing patterns on urban flooding is available to downtown planners from the geography department. Given Cork's moderate and compact size, UCC's involvement in this wider civic educational process gives a more concentrated *feel* of a university city than would be the case in Dublin.

Gown-town integration is also evident in the sphere of health and hospitals (there are now three 'university hospitals'). When the new, purpose-built University Dental School and Hospital was opened in Wilton in the early 1980s, the future of dentistry in Cork was assured, and the deciding factor was its necessity as a community health facility. The community dimension is also important in the food sciences, in computers and communications, and in the biosciences.

Today, urban merchants and commercial dons regard each other with mutual respect. President Tadhg Ó Ciardha (1978-88) was the first college head to realise the importance of embracing the whole business community and to promote connections between enterprises such as banks and individual college departments. A significant development was the establishment in UCC in 2004, under the aegis of the department of management and marketing, of the John C. Kelleher Family Business Centre in honour of Christy Kelleher, founder of Blarney Woollen Mills.[46] This new bond, between an academic department and a flourishing enterprise started by a self-made man, has a town-gown symbolism which would have greatly pleased a visionary college president like Bertram Windle.

In the recreational sphere, the completion of the splendid Mardyke Arena complex at the turn of the twenty-first century was a significant advance, not only in UCC sporting facilities but in the provision of health and recreational resources (notably, swimming and gymnasium) to the community at large.

Historically, the college has not had a strong social conscience extramurally but today it is keenly aware of its obligation to promote equality of educational opportunity in the local and regional community. The Access Programme[47] enables school leavers in designated disadvantaged schools to enter UCC and receive personal, academic and financial support in pursuing their studies and completing a degree. The college coaxes its network of graduates to help fund this flourishing access scheme. The good work commences at the primary level where the Bridging the Gap[48] programme encourages disadvantaged children through extracurricular activity to aspire to higher education, and to make a start by visiting the campus. These initiatives indicate a laudable social commitment to the goal of achieving a true university of the people.

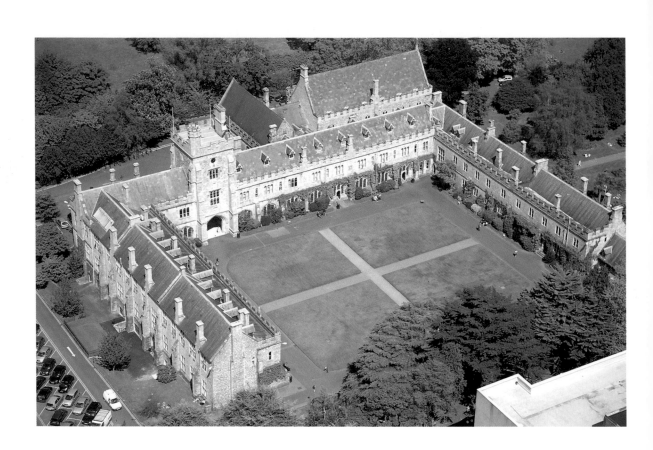

From the 1920s to the 1960s

UCC from the 1920s to the 1960s is often portrayed as provincial in the worst sense, smug, authoritarian and mediocre. But this is an unhistorical, selective and condescending view from a radically changed modern standpoint and it distorts the true picture. Even in the most reactionary academic periods, students resiliently enjoyed themselves and felt little sense of oppression. Escaping from the restrictions of home and secondary school, they experienced college as liberation and that was especially true in Ireland from the 1930s to the 1950s.

Though student numbers increased fairly steadily in the inter-war period (1919-39) they did so within a low range (500-1,000) so that the modest amenities available made life pleasant enough on a beautiful and uncrowded campus. 'Going to college' was the thing to do for the children of the well-off, and it had considerable cachet. *Aoibhinn beatha an scoláire*, says the *seanfhocal*, and the scholar's contentment was enhanced by the absence of the academic pressures of later decades. Entrance to the college did not present a scholastic challenge. The NUI matriculation examination made few demands on the average intelligence: where it did, friendly personators were informally available at a reasonable fee. A relaxed examination regimen within the college allowed for 'repeats' and for the phenomenon of the 'chronic' medical student. All that being said, students who worked hard fully deserved the honours grades they were awarded.

The appointment of senior academic staff was based on the votes of members of the governing body and of the university senate. While this system inevitably involved lobbying and cronyism, the number of blatantly unsuitable appointments was small.

Opposite:
Main Quadrangle

From the 1920s to the 1960s
From the 1920s to the

UCC in the mid-twentieth century had some remarkable scholars. Mention has been made of professors Busteed and Fleischmann. Another distinguished figure was James Hogan, professor of history 1920-63, who was a formative influence on the lives and careers of his students.[49] Daniel Corkery, writer, cultural philosopher and literary critic, was a national as well as a college intellectual presence. His appointment to the professorship of English (1931-47) was famously and unsuccessfully contested by his one-time protégé, Seán Ó Faoláin. Perhaps this experience coloured the disenchanted and jaundiced picture which Ó Faoláin draws of UCC in his auto-biography, *Vive Moi!*[50]

But the most dominant personality in UCC from the 1920s to the 1950s was the colourful Kerryman, Alfred O'Rahilly (1884-1969).[51] As registrar, he was the real power behind the presidential throne from 1920 to 1943. He served as president from 1943 to 1954, becoming a Holy Ghost priest on retirement though his influence was palpable in UCC into the early 1960s. (He was, incidentally, the last residential president, his house in the east wing becoming part of 'office' college after his departure.) He was a volatile and bustling polymath, 'a cross', it was observed, 'between Thomas Aquinas and Jimmy O'Dea'. He played an extraordinary number of extramural roles – social crusader, educationalist, political and social arbitrator, constitutional framer in 1922, Catholic Actionist, anti-communist polemicist, broadcaster, and popular journalist. His vast range of scholarly interests – politics, sociology, finance, Christology, math-ematical physics, history – provoked astonishment, criticism and ridicule. He challenged all things metropolitan, and particularly UCD's dominance in the National University of Ireland. His zeal for promoting a Catholic ethos in a nominally pluralist institution was paternalistic and authoritarian. A visiting examiner in the 1940s is reported to have described UCC as 'a convent run by a mad reverend mother'.

Yet, despite such caustic comments, and notwithstanding his absurd preoccupation with petty regulations (for example, his bizarre insistence that women students should wear stockings) and his generally unfavourable image in the college folklore, Alfred O'Rahilly was one of the most vibrant and effective presidents in the history of the

Left: Graduands processing across the Quad c.*1950's*

institution. His many initiatives included far-reaching improvements to the library and the provision of satisfactory health and restaurant services. He founded the electrical engineering department and the Cork University Press. He initiated the process whereby the adjoining county gaol site was transferred by the government to the college.[52] Initially, a 1-acre portion fronting College Road was handed over in 1946: here, the electrical engineering building was constructed and, here too, a monument was erected (at the side of what is now the main traffic entrance) over the graves of patriot volunteers who lost their lives during the War of Independence. After O'Rahilly's time, the remainder of the 3.5-acre gaol site was made over to (1957) and subsequently incorporated in the college, with the ugly but capacious science – now Kane – building being constructed in 1967-71, and the fine classical portico and front wall being preserved.

Previous page:
Students relaxing
in the President's
Garden

Thus, O'Rahilly not only provided for the growing accommodation needs of his own time, but initiated that remarkable westward expansion which has continued since then.

The 1950s in Ireland is generally seen as a dismal decade, characterised by social and economic stagnation. This national scene was reflected in UCC where the pleas of President Henry St J. Atkins (1954-63)[53] to the government to ameliorate the college's 'deplorable state financially' fell on deaf ears. Atkins had to operate a policy of financial conservatism and debt containment. In particular, the medical and dental schools were grossly underfunded. Atkins did well in staving off the shutdown of the dental school and in securing continuing recognition by British and American registration bodies of the medical school. Closing the dental school would have been very disappointing for Cork but there would have been some understanding of the hard expensive facts of training dentists. But fear of closure of the medical school was a nightmare which thankfully did not materialise. For all its social and dynastic elitism, the school was an indispensable component of the college, closely intertwined with its origins. Indeed, for some time at the turn of the twentieth century, it had virtually *been* the college.

The student revolution of the 1960s had a moderate and workmanlike expression in UCC.[54] Cork students were traditionally conservative: the middle-class campus and the local student intake favoured stability and tradition. Student power was expressed responsibly, taking the form of a constructive 'teach-in' in 1967 rather than quadrangle or street rioting. Still, the old deference was replaced by a new questioning. Increased fees (a 25 per cent jump in 1971-73, for example) and crowded accommodation (because of rapidly growing student numbers) were no longer fatalistically accepted. Protest took the form of office sit-ins, picketing of governing body meetings and even a lectures boycott but there was adjustment rather than sudden change in staff–student relations. The opening of the hitherto walled 'President's Garden' to the student body was hardly a revolutionary development (today, its delights are shared by photographed wedding groups from the nearby Honan Chapel). The ceasing of roll calls, the gradual discarding of staff and student gowns and a general sartorial relaxation, were all marks of a new informality. Lively debates in student societies polarised around domestic and international issues, censorship of topics and of speakers gradually disappeared, and so did the serried ranks of nuns and clerics. The growth in student numbers was a democratising factor since it helped to dilute elitism. But it was the introduction of student grants and the raising of entrance standards that effected some real measure of equality of opportunity.

Reform and Expansion

The modernising presidency of M.D. McCarthy (1967-78) brought belated reform and expansion to UCC.[55] As a graduate and former professor, McCarthy had an insider's feel for the place but as a public servant and administrator, he brought an outsider's experience and contacts back to the college. He had formidable intelligence, flinty integrity and a capacity for sustained hard work. Something of an administrative revolution now took place, causing intermittent complaints from academics that the new administrators were being too favourably treated. In fact, good administration meant that the academic staff got greatly improved facilities. The lynchpin figure here was the finance officer and secretary, Michael F. Kelleher, whose expertise over a long period (1974-2005) was of inestimable value to the college.

Under McCarthy, the appointments process was removed from the politicking of the governing body and entrusted to independent boards of assessors. The consequence was the ending of canvassing and localism, the raising of appointments standards and consequently of general college prestige. Moreover, a promotions system has encouraged academics to excel in their research and teaching. Like Windle earlier in the century, McCarthy favoured independent university status for UCC and the failure to realise this cherished hope was a great disappointment to him, as it had been to Windle.

Perhaps the principal McCarthy legacy, and the one which reflected his visionary approach, was the college development plan of 1972. This was a twenty-year plan of physical development around the original buildings, with an extended campus. The plan provided for a student population expanding from its 1972 base of about 4,000

Opposite:
Áras na Mac Léinn,
Student Centre

to a maximum of 7,000 twenty years ahead. Any substantial increase beyond that number, in McCarthy's view, would damage the distinctive character of UCC. Obviously, the plan had to be substantially modified in subsequent years but its broad lines remained valid. There was to be no second campus, though this mirage shimmered for a while in 1994 with the proposed acquisition of the vacated Our Lady's Hospital on the Lee Road, and a number of small centres would develop elsewhere. In the meantime, stability and continuity would be provided by expansion around the historic core. Successive building planners were to show great initiative and ingenuity in finding inner-campus development sites where, one would have thought, none existed.

Student numbers soared from 5,000 plus in 1980-81 to nearly 10,000 in 1993-94, as more and more school leavers (nationally, 11 per cent in 1965; 55 per cent in 2004) had access to higher education, with the aid of the grants system and, arguably, with the abolition in 1996, of undergraduate fees. Increasing numbers meant more teaching staff and ever-expanding courses in UCC as elsewhere. The demand for bigger lecturing areas, laboratory accommodation and office space had to be met. (Symbolically, some lecture rooms were retained in the quadrangle's west wing.) Accordingly, impressive building development was promoted by successive presidents – Tadhg Ó Ciardha (1978-88), Michael P. Mortell (1989-99) and Gerard T. Wrixon (1999–2007). Ó Ciardha once remarked that the sound of construction was music to his ears since it signified the burgeoning life of the college.

But where to find new building space and extra accommodation? The acquisition of private dwellings on the perimeter streets (Western Road, College Road) to be used as departmental locations could only be a partial and stopgap measure. The college had long wished to expand eastwards but opportunities in this direction seemed limited. A development on the Gillabbey Rock site would be in accordance with legend and tradition but City Hall firmly ruled this out on environmental grounds. (It was later ruefully recalled that, in the 1930s, the college had turned down what became the Jury's Hotel site, which was then on offer for £600!) But a very positive step was the acquisition in 1969 of the Lee Maltings, a former brewery premises near the Mercy

Hospital, a ten-minute walk from the main campus.[56] It was an unusual and successful move, providing the college with a badly needed book storage area, a recreational complex, more lecture halls and a new home for the department of zoology.

In time, an adjacent riverside building was to house a spectacularly successful enterprise, the National Microelectronics Research Centre (NMRC), under the direction of Professor Gerard T. Wrixon. It has been the face of UCC most associated in the public mind with scientific research successfully applied to high-tech business, very important for the national economy and creating substantial employment in its own right. A further major development was to take place in 2004 when substantial state funding was made available to upgrade the Lee Maltings complex and establish the Tyndall National Institute, providing extensive research facilities and incorporating the NMRC with photonics researchers at UCC and at the Cork Institute of Technology. Named after a noted nineteenth-century Irish scientist, it is a national focal point for excellence in research in these areas and related technologies.[57]

The eastern expansion also included the leasing or purchase of the former Presentation College premises on Western Road; the Eye, Ear and Throat Hospital; and the Cooperage and fine Georgian Distillery House, across the north channel from the Lee Maltings. A particularly significant development was the success of the Granary Theatre.[58] Originally housed as a stage premises for the UCC Dramatic Society in the granary section of the Lee Maltings, it was relocated in 1994 to an independent building on the Mardyke. Not only does it provide multidisciplinary programmes for Drama and Theatre Studies, but it is foremost in promoting experimental drama in the city, co-operating with community organisations and making a novel and exciting contribution to town–gown relationships.

However, the most important building initiative in the early 1980s was right in the heart of the old campus. This was the badly needed new library, built on the site of the old quarry between the Quadrangle and College Road.[59] (Nostalgic graduates were regretful about this as they recalled the muddily titanic sporting encounters in the Quarry during their student days.) Years in the planning, the splendid five-storey structure, with its underground complex of lecture halls and offices, opened in 1983 and was named after the mathematician George Boole, the most renowned professor (1849-64) in the history of the institution. The Boole Library once more exemplified

The final whistle!
Match in the
Quarry, 1977

the resourcefulness of college planners in finding new locations. The building grace-fully completed the unfinished symphony of the quadrangle, with the ancient trees on the embankment acting effectively as an aesthetically pleasing screen. In the early 2000s, further space was found, almost incredibly, for a new postgraduate library on the eastern flank of the Boole. Five storeys over an excavated basement added 60 per cent to the existing space, and this fully equipped extension was two-thirds funded by Atlantic Philanthropies, American benefactors already more than generous to UCC.

From the 1980s, the vacated old library building in the north wing behind the Quadrangle now served two new purposes, the ground floor becoming a comfortable staff common room with the floor above accommodating various council meetings (including those of the governing body). Meanwhile, hungry students' needs were met by an extension to the main restaurant and by café services elsewhere on campus.

Westward expansion continued, beyond the Kane Building and the Gaol Walk. La Retraite, a hall of residence for women students (1923-77) was acquired by UCC, renamed Áras na Laoi, and modernised and greatly extended to accommodate various departments, lecture rooms and the audio-visual unit.[60] Another major undertaking was the Dairy and Food Science building for which M.D. McCarthy laid a commemoration stone in 1978 in one of the last acts of his presidency. It was enhanced by a large extension in 1993: thus, what had been a major strength of UCC from the 1920s now became a national and international centre of excellence through its different specialities. Across the valley in Sunday's Well, the purchase of the capacious Good Shepherd Convent held out promising prospects, not least as a location for the music department, but misfortune dogged the premises before it was finally disposed of: music has found a satisfactory home in part of the St Vincent's Church complex, further east in Sunday's Well.

Millennium Developments

In reviewing the 1972 plan and taking account of other developments, the governing body in July 1993, agreed that, in President Mortell's words, 'our revised plan when fully implemented, will result in a compact unified campus based on the existing college grounds and in continued harmony with its urban location'. Two new major projects to the east of the Quadrangle were in line with this policy. The Devere Hall/Áras na Mac Léinn, built in 1995 and further refined thereafter, is a student centre funded by a special levy on students' fees but named after an American benefactor.[61] It centralises many student services including a travel office and the campus radio station. The great multifunctional hall is a welcome facility, available for large-scale graduations, banquets and various assemblies. The impressive glass frontage of the Áras seems full of reflections, enhancing the sense of spaciousness and light. Like the matching O'Rahilly Building across the new, attractive Honan Square, its many windows afford delightfully unexpected vistas of the undulating urban landscape nearby. In addition to the Boole/Restaurant area, Áras na Mac Léinn is a lively hub of student congregation.

The O'Rahilly Building (1997) is a major structure, situated in the southeast of the campus bloc, where the men's residential Honan Hostel used to be. This new edifice is a splendid architectural composition, all glittering blocks of limestone and glass. It provides offices and lecture/seminar rooms for a wide range of disciplines in the humanities and social sciences, previously and unsuitably accommodated in college-acquired houses on the campus periphery. The appropriately named building recalls the wide scholarly interests of a remarkable president whose career is sketched on an impressive commemorative tablet in the foyer.

Opposite: Brookfield Health Science Complex

The physical and academic progress of UCC continued apace under the leadership of President Wrixon. (It might be noted that of the seven universities in the State, UCC has the smallest acreage in its ownership.) The School of Pharmacy was established in 2003 with a mission to produce graduates in both community pharmacy and in the pharmaceutical industry. The school is housed on College Road in the new Cavanagh Pharmacy Building, which also contains a postgraduate research area. This state-of-the art building is named after businessman Tom Cavanagh, graduate, governor, benefactor and committed UCC activist. Still farther west off College Road is the magnificent Brookfield complex,[62] the new home for the Schools of Medicine, Nursing and Therapies, aesthetically incorporating the old Jennings firebrick residence into the structure. The Brookfield project maximises the integrated education of health professionals through shared facilities and staff. The Environmental Research Institute at the Lee Road on the banks of the river, and a purpose-built IT building at the former greyhound track on the Western Road, are two other important developments.

The purchase of the Mardyke Gardens (2003) provided a key strategic site. The simple yet elegant Mardyke pedestrian bridge[63] which the City Council built in 2005 affords a scenic cross-river route to new and old buildings in UCC's North Mall complex – the Departments of Zoology, Ecology and Plant Science and the Department of Applied Psychology, all transferred from other college locations. There is

Opposite: Honan Square

now an impressive cluster of university buildings on both sides of the north channel near the Mercy University Hospital.

Whatever other developments UCC might have in mind in the Mardyke-North Mall area would have to take into account City Hall's obligations to preserve precious open riverside space. However, in this general respect, town-gown relations are harmonious. City Hall greatly appreciates UCC's significant role in the urban economy and it is anxious to facilitate the university's further expansion eastwards.[64] But when

72

urban planners hint at a future academic presence in the docklands area, UCC may well find that a step too far!

The BioSciences Institute,[65] immediately to the west of Áras na Laoi, is another extensive ultra-modern building, dedicated to multidisciplinary research in the biomedical sciences. Teamwork, sharing funding and equipment, and collaboration with industry are the hallmarks of the institute where the researchers have international experience and contacts.

Above:
Department of Music
(St Vincent's Church)
overlooking the
Mardyke Pedestrian
Bridge

An exciting new departure in 2004 was the setting up of the BioTransfer Unit (BTU). This is responsible for the management of the BioInnovation Centre on the third floor of the Food Science building where refurbished laboratory facilities provide the basis for the establishment of spin-out BioTech campus companies. The idea is that researchers and entrepreneurs approach the BTU with ideas they believe would have a commercial application. Once approved, they move into the BioInnovation Centre as 'client' companies, and are given tenure for a maximum of three years. The centre gives these fledgling companies a sheltered environment and an encouraging university research milieu. This novel scheme encourages research-driven entrepreneurship. The centre will support up to six spin-off companies at any given time and has the potential to create hundreds of jobs.[66]

The shining pride of all the new millennium buildings is the Lewis Glucksman Gallery, a personal initiative of President Wrixon.[67] When the idea of a purpose-built art gallery and riverside restaurant in the Lower Grounds was first mooted, some academics were apprehensive. It was felt that the tranquillity of this parkland

Right: Tennis tournament in the Lower Grounds, 1917 Opposite: The Lewis Glucksman Gallery is built on the 'footprint' of the former tennis courts

area, cherished by generations of students, would be so compromised that its very ambience would be destroyed. In the event, such fears proved groundless. The 'footprint' of the new building was no bigger than the tennis court and shabby wooden pavilion, which had long occupied the city end of the secluded grounds. Not alone is there no further encroachment on the existing space but the stunning new structure enhances the grounds and the approaches in entirely unexpected ways.

It presents the appearance of a series of limestone and glass boxes around a central axis: a great curving wooden structure, punctuated with windows, is cantilevered out from the main building and rests on slender stilts. Two large galleries give a striking sense of presence and space. Overall, the Gallery manages to blend in with, as well as stand out from, its surroundings of mature trees. The Lewis Glucksman Gallery was sponsored by a wealthy New Yorker and his third-generation Irish-American wife, Loretta Brennan Glucksman, and it was opened in October 2004 by Mary McAleese, President of Ireland.

This marvellously imaginative structure, already acclaimed by awards, is itself a work of art. Situated at the most accessible point of the college to the city, it belongs to town as much as to gown, it adds significantly to the visual arts amenities of the area, and it will play no small part in developing the artistic sensibilities of Cork and Munster children. Apart from the Glucksman Gallery, there is increasing involvement in the visual arts on the part of academic staff and individual departments.

One of the great social changes in the lives of UCC students in the late twentieth century concerned residential accommodation. Those not living at home could number, at any given time, half the student body. Closely supervised halls of residence (separated by gender) and approved 'digs' with motherly landladies now belong to a bygone authoritarian age. The demise of such (Catholic) hostels as La Retraite and the Honan took place when their original rationale became out of joint with the new secularised times. Deanships of residence, going back to the early Queen's College days, have long since been abolished, and the women's dean quaintly acting the role of chaperone is but a fading memory.

Modern out-of-town students now live in increasing numbers in unsupervisable rental houses and apartments. The deteriorating appearance of some houses in student-residential streets adjacent to the campus is a matter of environmental concern. Substantial student residences in the shape of self-catering apartments have been built by the college itself and by commercial interests: local residents are sometimes unhappy about the design and location of such 'high-rises'. Castlewhite (1991) on the campus has been followed by Victoria Lodge, Farranlea Hall and the Spires, all reasonably near, all owned or leased by UCC, and together accounting for a substantial minority of non-home based students. (During vacation, student residences double as accommodation centres for campus conferences, summer schools and the tourist trade). The college also monitors the accommodation standards of other students not under its direct aegis. In all cases, however, the supervisory interest is concerned only with the comfort, safety and health of students and no longer with their moral behaviour. The transition from supervised, denominational residential accommodation to an independent, secular and largely unsupervised mode of student living, reflects the radical social changes in Irish life at large.

All civilised institutions must cherish their past as well as plan for their future. The task of the Heritage Committee, set up in the late 1990s, is to make the university community aware of the individuals who have helped to shape its history, and to preserve and restore the physical heritage. (This writer had the privilege of being the first chair of the committee.) It is UCC policy to commemorate, where possible, significant figures from the past by naming or renaming buildings in their honour, though hard financial realities dictate that present-day benefactors, often unconnected with the place, must sometimes be included in the naming process. Name signs and information tablets have been put in place, for example, commemorating Kane, Boole, Windle and O'Rahilly, on particular buildings associated with their individual disciplines or achievements. The impressive refurbishment of the Aula Maxima has already been mentioned, as has the restorative work on the Crawford Observatory. Another major undertaking has been the conservation, reorganisation and rearrangment

Above:
UCC's twenty-
eight Ogam stones
are the largest
collection on display
in Ireland and are
a priceless part of
Ireland's national
heritage

of the display of the college's unique collection – the largest in Ireland – of ogam stones, in the north (Stone Corridor) and west cloisters of the Quadrangle.[68] It should be noted that student familiarity over the decades with these antique stones on open display has not, happily, resulted in any major defacement or damage.

In all this process of assuring continuity in an area of rapid change, the roles of the university archivist and of the university curator are invaluable. In instituting such posts, UCC once again took a pioneering lead.

Financing has been a problem, and a constant preoccupation of college administrators, from the beginning. In recent decades, governments have made it clear that universities, more and more, will have to help generate funding. University funding also has a political dimension. Many would argue that the abolition of undergraduate fees in 1996 was a political expedient and did little to redress educational inequality,[69] student maintenance costs being a more critical factor than fees. However, it should be added that there is now a clear government commitment to significant university funding.[70] It should also be stated that the national percentage of socio-economically disadvantaged children entering third-level education has been increasing dramatically in the last two decades or so.[71]

UCC spends considerable resources in maintaining touch with its legion of graduates, through glossy publications such as the *UCC Graduate*. The hope is that reasonably well-off graduates, animated by loyalty and gratitude to their alma mater, will help with one or other of several key projects through tax-efficient donations.

Universities Act: Controversy

While not as obviously significant a landmark as the 1908 Irish Universities Act, the 1997 Universities Act will be seen in time to have been a turning point in the history of the college. From 1908, UCC had enjoyed quasi-independent status under some federal restraint but the new act made UCD, UCG, Maynooth and Cork fully independent constituent universities of the NUI, masters of their own destiny, deciding their own courses and examination standards, and making their own appointments from the presidency downwards. The NUI Senate in Dublin would retain a co-ordinating role, direct the external examining system, deal with the awarding of prizes and fellowships, decide on the recipients of honorary degrees, and act as a forum for debates on educational policies. Each constituent university was entitled to style itself 'National University of Ireland' followed by the name of the particular campus. Cork, however, chose not to use 'NUI Cork' as its primary description but rather to retain its familiar UCC name. To some, this seemed a perverse decision, given the fulfilment, at last, of an aspiration cherished from Windle's time down to McCarthy's. Yet the retention was justified not so much on grounds of sentiment and tradition as on the practical basis of recognition of 'the brand name'. UCD took a similar line but Galway and Maynooth exulted in their new names as well as their independent status.

Professor Gerard T. Wrixon[72] was the first president to direct UCC in its fully independent phase (the 1997 legislation greatly enhanced presidential power). He was also the first president to be appointed by an independent committee on an internationally based search-and-selection system, with no reference to the sounding

Opposite: Western Avenue approach

out of academic staff opinion, to votes, or to the counting of heads at any level. Essentially, this was the process already in place for academic posts, so that any fears that total Cork control might mean localism or favouritism[73] were groundless. But some academics looking at a determined new president, at a reconstituted governing body with strong business interests, and at a terminology which tended to use the language of the boardroom, were apprehensive that a top-down corporate governance would adversely affect the ethos of a university as a community of scholars, inspired by collegial responsibility.

Wrixon's vigorous approach did not make him universally popular with the academic community. A proposal (eventually successful) to extend his tenure of office beyond the usual retirement age caused controversy. The atmosphere was further aggravated by a motion (eventually withdrawn) from a 'lay' governor that an academic who publicly took the lead in criticising Wrixon's policies and procedures be removed from the governing body. Wrixon's critics also drew attention to UCC's financial position, but the president was adamant that the college overdraft was 'absolutely manageable' and no cause for concern. With characteristic forcefulness, he denounced what he regarded as 'a handful of people that are content to remain unambitious and who would not feel at all out of place in a mediocre institution'. [74]

For the future historian of UCC in the early 2000s, the voluminous exchange of e-mails between academic staff on these issues will provide a lively and characteristically modern source for an analysis of this outbreak of *odium academicum*.[75] This is a virulent, if thankfully intermittent, fever which has raged everywhere in the groves of academe from time to time (Cork being no exception) and which often presents its unedifying face to a curious public. In 1994, for example, a clash between the then president (Michael P. Mortell) and registrar (Michael A. Moran) was as distracting and divisive as it was, in retrospect, incomprehensible.[76]

In the early twenty-first century, UCC was foremost in securing research funding and could claim to be Ireland's leading research institution. A vice-president for research policy aimed even higher:

> We will know we have reached our full potential when excellent
> staff from overseas choose to relocate to UCC, when our staff
> are being headhunted by overseas universities, when excellent
> students from overseas choose UCC for their research training
> and when UCC postgraduates and research outputs are in
> demand across the world.[77]

Perhaps such enthusiasm was not universally shared. Where financing was concerned, teaching seemed to be the poor relation, with unsatisfactory staff–student
ratios. Some academics also worried that research (by which was generally meant
science-related research) might become too responsive to the demands of governments, business and the 'knowledge-based economy'; that the university might be in
danger of becoming an institute of higher scientific technology; and that the
humanities might be seen as irrelevant, and go to the wall. That is why, in UCC
plans for further postgraduate expansion from 2005, a balancing mechanism was
introduced: this was 'the president's scholarship' for a PhD exclusively in arts,
commerce or law.

A projection[78] of further substantial growth in student numbers in the 2004-05
to 2010-11 period, from 15,500 to 21,000, would entail substantial extra budgeting
and would necessarily require additional building space, probably on the city end
of a campus that was now spectacularly developing on a west–east spine from the
old Greyhound Track to the Distillery Fields. Future student growth would
heavily favour the postgraduate sector, the argument being that it was this so-called
fourth-level which would ultimately decide the reputation and status of the
university. Thus, undergraduate quotas would remain unchanged except for
'mature' and 'access' students where UCC would continue to observe its obligation
to give special help to late starters and the socially underprivileged. But postgraduate numbers would be doubled from 2,920 to 6,060, with a significant
increase in the number of PhD students. The ceiling of 7,000 students overall,
envisaged in the early 1970s by President McCarthy, has long since been broken
through and the graph that had curved upwards from the 1960s would now reach for
the stars.

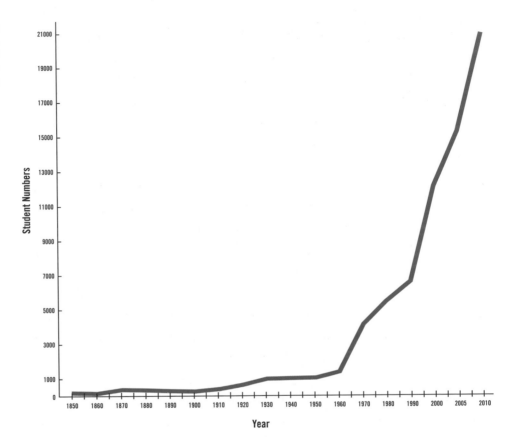

Increasingly, the UCC student body is culturally diverse in composition.[79] Even in the immediate post-World War II period, there was an impressive sprinkling of foreign students – Poles (former 'freedom fighters') and Africans mostly – amounting to a surprising 6 per cent of the total number. From the 1980s, European Union-sponsored arrangements such as Erasmus, as well as so-called exchange programmes with US universities (originating in UCC international summer schools from the late 1970s) brought welcome numbers of foreign students to the campus. This cosmopolitan flavour has been further enhanced by the presence of students from the Middle East, India and the Far East, particularly from China.[80] Non-EU students generate a multimillion euro fee revenue for the university, especially in the medical faculty. Sixty per cent of medical places, nationally, were taken up by overseas students

Opposite:
Western Road gate

in 2004. (Early in 2006, the government announced plans to more than double medical places for Irish and EU students over a four-year period.)

In 2004, seventy-five different nationalities were represented in UCC, comprising about 12 per cent of the student body. Apart from bringing obvious economic benefits, foreign students modify ingrained provincialism and open up the university and the city to stimulatingly diverse cultural influences. In turn, many of the visitors take a close interest in Irish studies.

In the early years of the twenty-first century, in UCC as elsewhere, a modernising president met with some opposition from traditionalist academics on the issue of 'restructuring' the internal university framework.[81] The proposal to regroup faculty structures into new 'colleges' (a confusing term, given the retention of the colloquial 'college' to denote UCC) was suspect to those who feared that the process was a further manifestation of the managerial ethos, of autocratic interference from on high, and of erosion of faculty rights.

There would be four colleges, each directed by a powerful executive head: Arts, Celtic Studies and Social Sciences; Business and Law; Science, Engineering and Food Sciences; and Medicine and Health. This radical change was intended to enhance research and teaching and to make optimum use of resources which would be devolved to the new colleges. A Resources Allocation Model would be a critical mechanism in achieving this. The system would aim at greater flexibility in the allocation of resources, more emphasis on the cross-disciplinary dimension and wider student choices. It was hoped that there would be a reduction in the size of the central administration and greater academic involvement in decision-making. Overall, the four heads of colleges would be members of the key University Management Group.

If restructuring worked successfully, it would meet the genuine concerns, rather than fulfil the worst fears, of traditionalists. However, it was not clear to everyone how the new system would affect the standing of existing structures – the faculty, enshrined in statute, or eventually, the department, the basic academic unit commanding staff loyalty. Only time would answer other questions. For example, was the grouping of faculties more a matter of administrative convenience, rather than based on a genuine academic rationale?

The Eternal Student

UCC was chosen by *The Sunday Times* as the Irish University of the year for 2003,[82] and again for 2005.[83] This signal recognition was awarded for a number of reasons – the university's position as the leading research institution in Ireland; its cosmopolitan character with an admirable student mix; the excellence of its teaching and academic standards; the flexibility of its degree programmes; its low drop-out rates; its high level of graduate employment; its links with business and industry; and its successful Access and Bridging the Gap programmes.

But in the last analysis, the student is at the heart of everything, and what uniquely characterises a university, as distinct either from a research institute *simpliciter* or a business concern, is the relationship between student and lecturer, and that has been the case since universities began.

The quality of the student experience is a very important factor in determining the award of excellence to a university. The student's lot in UCC in the early twenty-first century may not be an ecstatically happy one – overcrowding on the campus, inadequate maintenance grants and (sometimes) substandard and overpriced accommodation are frequent complaints. On the whole, however, students are better cared for than at any previous period. (UCC has taken the lead in Ireland in looking after students with disabilities.) College restaurant services are reasonably good, students are well represented on various college bodies, an ever-increasing variety of undergraduate courses and of postgraduate disciplines offer every possible academic fulfilment, and the proliferation of student clubs and societies (130 plus in 2005-06) caters for general as well as specialist recreational interests. And the long vacation

Opposite: Clock Tower

(the lecturing year is shorter than ever) and cheap air fares enable students to see the world and/or earn spending money for the next session, in ways that were simply unthinkable for their predecessors: for one thing, physical or even clerical work during long holidays was not deemed socially acceptable for the genteel students of the first half of the twentieth century.

For whatever reasons, student protests, marches and demos (let alone riots) seemed to be in abeyance in the decades around the new millennium. What accounted for this lapse in a time-honoured tradition? Perhaps it was because there were no serious grievances on campus, and the individualist ethos of the age may have dulled the edge of social conscience where the injustices of the nation or of the wider world were concerned.

The founding fathers of Queen's College Cork were well aware that the new institution, in the hallowed tradition of Finbarr's school of learning (as they perceived it), could not live apart from the city and the province. But it would take more than a century for that belief to become a meaningful reality. In part, it was the transformed

ambience of Cork and Munster that made the college eventually realise its potential. The prosperous and creative city of the early 2000s manifested itself in the arts as well as in the economy and that was also reflected in UCC. The college responded successfully to the challenges posed by a thriving Cork Institute of Technology and a vibrant new university in Limerick to its erstwhile monopoly of third-level education in the city and the province. The cream of Cork students in the region – perhaps the top 15 per cent – made UCC the university of their choice because of its perceived excellence.

What also distinguishes today's UCC is its ceaseless and multi-faceted activity. Evening degree courses, public lectures and various student activities fill the night-time hours. Even during vacation, many students remain on campus, read in the library and socialise in the restaurants. In-service courses, miscellaneous conferences, adult education sessions, teaching-English-to-foreigners classes and thriving international summer schools – all keep lecture halls occupied, residential apartments full, the university coffers topped up and the contract caterers smiling. However, despite the best efforts of the campus communications office, many citizens still cling to the outdated image of UCC as a leisurely 1930s place of dilettantish dalliance.

Finally, today's students and academic staff are children of the computer age and, through the internet, have global access at their fingertips. It is in this respect more than any other that UCC transcends the limitations of its provincial geography. Cork and Munster are still learning where Finbarr, whoever he was, reputedly taught. That much is continuity. All else is change.

Seekers of Knowledge, *bronze statue by Annette Hennessy, 1994, (near Civil Engineering Building)*

Notes

1. John A. Murphy, *The College: A History of Queen's/University College Cork* (hereinafter *College*), (Cork, 1995), p. 1.
2. At a QCC prize-giving ceremony on 27 November 1857: *President's Report*, 1856-57, p. 44.
3. *College*, p. 18.
4. *Ibid.*, p. 5.
5. *Ibid.*, p. 6.
6. Dr D.B. Bullen, testimony to the Wyse Committee, 1835-38, quoted in *College*, p. 7.
7. See my entries on the RCI and the CCS in *The Encyclopaedia of Ireland*, ed. Brian Lalor (Dublin, 2003), pp. 238-39 and 945; also Kieran MacCarthy, 'The Royal Cork Institution', in *Atlas of Cork City*, ed. J.S. Crowley *et al.* (Cork, 2005), pp. 223-27.
8. Chief Secretary's Office Registered Papers (CSORP) 1845, no. 6766, National Archives of Ireland (NAI).
9. For this paragraph, see *College*, pp. 11-12, 17.
10. *Ibid.*, p. 13.
11. *Ibid.*, pp. 11-13.
12. *Ibid.*, pp. 21ff.
13. T.B. Macaulay, *The History of England from the Accession of James II* (London, 1906), vol. II, p. 344.
14. CSORP 1875, no. 4629, NAI.
15. *The Cork Examiner* (hereinafter *CE*) 26 September 1849.
16. *College*, pp. 30-31.
17. Frederick O'Dwyer, *The Architecture of Deane and Woodward* (Cork, 1997) pp. 72ff; *University College Cork: A Portrait in Words and Images* (hereinafter *Portrait*): text by John A. Murphy, images by Andrew Bradley (Cork, 2005), pp. 22-27.

18. *CE*, 26 September and 7 November 1849.

19. John A. Murphy, 'Opening of Queen's College Cork', *UCC Graduate* 2000.

20. *College*, pp. 39-42.

21. *Ibid.*, p. 386.

22. John A. Murphy, 'The College and The Gaol', 2002 *Graduate Review*, pp. 92-95; *College*, pp. 62-64.

23. *College*, Appendix D, pp. 389-92.

24. For Kane's presidency, see *ibid* ch. 4.

25. CSORP 1862, no. 14733, NAI.

26. For Sullivan's presidency, see *College*, ch. 5.

27. 'New life for Observatory', 2002 *Graduate Review*, pp. 64-66; 'Star Graduates', *UCC News*, October 2004, pp. 14-15; 'Sky Watching', *UCC News*, November 2005.

28. *College*, ch. 6.

29. *Ibid.*, pp. 122-23, 141-45.

30. *Ibid.*, ch. 7, 'The Windle Era', pp. 24, 26, 28.

31. *UCC News*, November 2004, p. 17.

32. Virginia Teehan and Elizabeth Wincott Heckett, *The Honan Chapel: A Golden Vision* (Cork, 2004); Mary Leland, *The Honan Chapel: A Guide* (Cork, 2004).

33. *College*, pp. 222ff.

34. John A. Murphy, 'Cork University Press in Context', CUP Anniversary Catalogue 1925-2000, pp. 37-44.

35. *Portrait*, pp. 12-13, 16-17. For an expert comment on the UCC St Finbarr statue, see Ann Wilson, *Séamus Murphy, 1907–1975, Sculptor*, ed. Peter Murray (Cork, 2007), pp. 32–33.

36. Pádraig Ó Riain, 'St Finbarr: a study in a cult', *Journal of the Cork Historical and Archaeological Society*, 82 (1977), pp. 63-82.

37. *CE*, 19 April 1913.

38. *CE*, 5 November 1926.

39. *College*, pp. 250ff.

40. See, in general, *College*, ch. 9, 'The Many Sides of Town and Gown'.

41. *CE*, 17 December 1928.

42. *College*, pp. 252-54.

43. See below, n. 51.

44. *Aloys Fleishmann (1910-92)*, ed. Ruth Fleischmann (Cork, 2000), including my own tribute, pp. 215-19.

45. *College*, pp. 336-39.

46. See *Irish Examiner*, 21 May 2004.

47. 'UCC Diary', *Evening Echo*, 29 March 2004, p. 14.

48. *The College Courier*, Winter 2003, pp. 8-9.

49. See *James Hogan, Revolutionary, Historian, and Political Scientist*, ed. Donnchadh Ó Corráin (Dublin, 2001), including my own tribute, pp. 35-38.

50. *College*, pp. 227-32; John A. Murphy 'Daniel Corkery', in *RIA Dictionary of Irish Biography*, (Cambridge University Press, forthcoming).

51. *College*, pp. 270ff; John A. Murphy 'Alfred O'Rahilly', in *RIA Dictionary of Irish Biography* (Cambridge University Press, forthcoming).

52. *College*, pp. 290-92.

53. *Ibid.*, pp. 292-97.

54. *Ibid.*, pp. 311ff.

55. *Ibid.*, pp. 320-32

56. *Ibid.*, pp. 334-35.

57. *UCC News*, January 2005 and February 2006; *The Irish Times* (*IT*) 23 February 2006; *Portrait,* pp. 44-45.

58. *Portrait*, pp. 98-99.

59. *College*, pp. 329-30.

60. *Portrait*, p. 46.

61. *Ibid.*, pp. 82-83.

62. See account of opening, *IT*, Health Supplement, 29 November 2005.

63. See *Irish Examiner*, 2 February 2006.

64. See *Cork City Council: Cork City Development Plan 2004*, Vol. 1, Main Strategy, esp. pp. 167-68.

65. *UCC Graduate 2004*, pp. 36-37; *Portrait*, pp. 42-43.

66. Gerald Fitzgerald, 'Spinning Out', *UCC News*, October 2004; 'Making the leap form R&D to business', *IT*, 16 November 2005.

67. Fiona Kearney, Director, 'Glucksman Celebrations', *UCC Graduate*, 2004, pp. 2-6; *Portrait*, pp. 76-79.

68. 'Treasures of the Stone Corridor', *The College Courier*, Winter 2003, pp. 2-3; Damian

McManus, *The Ogam Stones at UCC* (Cork, 2004).

69. For a different view, see article by James Wrynn, *IT*, 20 March 2006.

70. See *IT*, 12 December 2005.

71. See *Who Went to College in 2004? A National Survey of New Entrants to Higher Education* by P.J. O'Connell *et al.* (Higher Education Authority, 2006).

72. See interview, *UCC News*, June 2004, pp. 1-3.

73. Such fears had long been expressed by, for example, Professor Aloys Fleishmann. See *College*, p. 323 and n. 19 on p. 436.

74. Interview, *UCC News*, June 2006. In the event Wrixon did not complete his extended term, announcing that he would retire in January 2007.

75. See my discussion on this, *College*, p. 225.

76. *College*, p. 360.

77. Vice-President for Research Policy and Support, Peter Kennedy, 'Planning Ahead', *UCC Graduate 2005*, p. 27; also see Kevin Collins, 'Leading the Way at UCC' (overview of scientific research) *UCC Graduate 2004*, pp. 26-27.

78. Vice-President for Planning, Communications and Development, Michael O'Sullivan, *UCC Strategic Plan 2006-2011*, presented to the governing body, 4 October 2005.

79. See for example, 'UCC's Global Reach' *UCC Graduate, 2004*, pp. 7-9; also, *Portrait*, pp. 84-85.

80. See *Portrait*, pp. 86-87.

81. See 'Restructuring Now' *UCC News*, February 2005, pp. 1-3. President Wrixon's restructuring proposals were endorsed by the governing body on 21 June, 2005.

82. *The College Courier*, Winter 2003.

83. *Irish Examiner*, 1 October 2005.

Index

Please note that Mc is treated the same as Mac. Page numbers in italics indicate an illustration or caption.

Opposite page:
Fantailled on the Falls,
stainless steel and
bronze sculpture by
Conor Fallon, 1995/6 on
wall of student centre.